KT-159-827

THE MAMMOTH BOOK OF
MIXED MARTIAL ARTS

Over 400 Photographs in Bone-crunching Detail

RUNNING PRESS
PHILADELPHIA · LONDON

ROBINSON

Constable & Robinson Ltd
3 The Lanchesters
162 Fulham Palace Road
London W6 9ER
www.constablerobinson.com

First published in the UK by Robinson,
an imprint of Constable & Robinson, 2011

Copyright in photographs and text © Lee Whitehead, 2011

The right of Lee Whitehead to be identified as the
author of this work has been asserted by him in accordance
with the Copyright, Designs & Patents Act 1988.

All rights reserved. This book is sold subject to the condition
that it shall not, by way of trade or otherwise, be lent, re-sold,
hired out or otherwise circulated in any form of binding or cover
other than that in which it is published and without a similar condition
including this condition being imposed on the subsequent purchaser.

A copy of the British Library Cataloguing in Publication
Data is available from the British Library

UK ISBN 978-1-84529-945-3

1 3 5 7 9 10 8 6 4 2

First published in the United States in 2011 by Running Press Book Publishers

All rights reserved under the Pan-American and International Copyright
Conventions

This book may not be reproduced in whole or in part, in any form or by any
means, electronic or mechanical, including photocopying, recording, or by any
information storage and retrieval system now known or hereafter invented,
without written permission from the publisher.

9 8 7 6 5 4 3 2 1
Digit on the right indicates the number of this printing

US Library of Congress number: 2010940268
US ISBN 978-0-7624-4119-8

Running Press Book Publishers
2300 Chestnut Street
Philadelphia, PA 19103-4371

Visit us on the web!
www.runningpress.com

Printed and bound in China

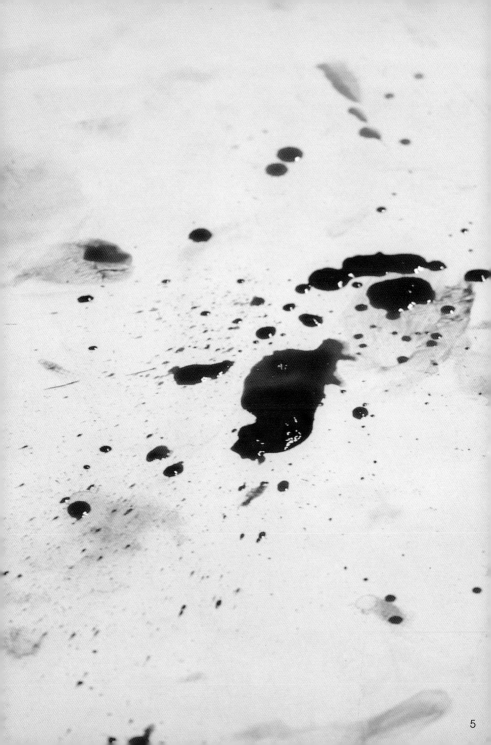

LEE WHITEHEAD
AUTHOR / PHOTOGRAPHER

INTRODUCTION

Where *Blunt Force Trauma* had a particular story to tell – the concept of Mixed Martial Arts – this book aims to enhance awareness of the sport by providing a greater insight into the fighters who step into the cage and put their bodies on the line.

It always surprises me when I speak to people who are alien to the sport and have pre-conceived ideas that bear little or no resemblance to what actually goes on. They do not view the fighters as athletes, but merely as thugs who compete in some kind of underground 'Fight Club' where the battle rages until an eyeball rolls across the floor.

The reality is that these sportsmen and women are tough, dedicated individuals who all possess the singularity of mind to pursue their goals and test themselves in the cage. Some are undefeated, others are stuck in a run of tough losses, but they all train hard in order to chase victory.

Mixed Martial Arts is a community, and top-flight fighters train at the same places as the enthusiast or the yearly warrior – further dispelling the notion that MMA is a kind of underground movement. Fighters are some of the most down-to-earth, friendly and gracious people you could meet; of course, there are exceptions, but on the whole getting hit in the face and humbled on the mat has a way of keeping even the most flamboyant of characters grounded when away from the prying eye of the cameras.

I do hope you enjoy this book and see it as brief but nevertheless enlightening snapshot of the sport, its players, and its injuries and challenges.

Matt Ewin / Mark Epstein

FIGHTER PROFILES

Christian Smith

Slamming your way out of an armbar can be effective on occasion, but it's not the best form of defence you can employ. Prevention is better – leaving your arm in to begin with.

Karsten Lenjoint (right) kept fishing for submissions in his fight with Chris Trowton (left) at the fifth Enter the Rough House show in Nottingham. Several armbars were slapped on good and tight, but it was a triangle that eventually secured victory!

Evangelista Santos

Mike Ling / Carl Noon

Born:	July 1st, 1979
Nationality:	American
Height:	6' 3"
Weight:	205lbs
Division:	Light Heavyweight
Nickname:	The Original Ultimate Fighter

Forrest Griffin made a huge impression on me when I first saw his fights at the IFC: Global Domination shows back in 2003 – submitting Chael Sonnen with a tight triangle and sticking it to tough veteran Jeremy Horn before being taken out of the game by a brutal head kick knockout.

His time on *The Ultimate Fighter* is well documented and his fight at the season finale with Stephan Bonner is a thing of modern MMA legend, but it's his personality and balls-to-the-wall fighting style that endear him to fans.

Every time I have met him he has been more than willing to give up his time and chat about anything that comes into his or my mind.

Whatever his achievements with the UFC, be it holding the Light Heavyweight title once again or having brutal, bloody fights, he will always be looked upon as the original 'tuffer who done good'.

And to think that prior to going on the show he almost walked away from the sport entirely.

FORREST GRIFFIN

Born:	January 4th, 1975
Nationality:	American
Height:	6' 2"
Weight:	265lbs
Division:	Heavyweight
Nickname:	The Engineer

Shane Carwin is a monster of a man and one of only a few fighters on the same size scale as incumbent UFC Heavyweight Champion Brock Lesnar. He is also a former foe of the ex-WWE wrestler, having given the fighter a lot of trouble during their encounter with the power punches he threw.

Fortunately for Lesnar, the challenger succumbed to his exertions in the second round and yielded to an arm-triangle submission, marking the first professional loss of his career. Ever gracious, Carwin acknowledged his error and is already working back to contention.

Jason Barrett has a bulging haematoma examined between rounds.

Sixty seconds is a very short time to take instruction on board, have a cut dealt with and catch your breath.

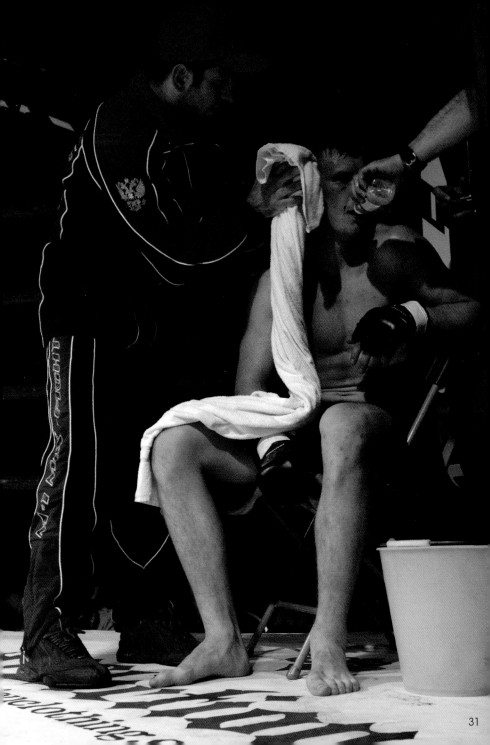

Leonard Garcia

Rob Broughton

Born:	May 17th, 1982
Nationality:	English
Height:	6' 0"
Weight:	170lbs
Division:	Welterweight
Nickname:	The Outlaw

Dan Hardy is a love- or hate-type fighter: he is outspoken, brash and one of the sharpest verbal takedown merchants in the game, but he is also a shrewd operator who understands that media, marketing and psychological warfare are all part of the sport.

With Mixed Martial Arts in continual ascension, there is a risk that fighters can become anodyne, flavourless clones of each other. To be able to stand out clearly from the pack as an individual requires a alchemic mix of skills and savvy, of which he has both in spades.

Former Cage Warriors dual-weight class champion, veteran of over twenty-five fights and former challenger to the UFC Welterweight title held by Georges St-Pierre. Hardy has come a long was since the early days where he worked as a personal trainer while developing his fledgling MMA career.

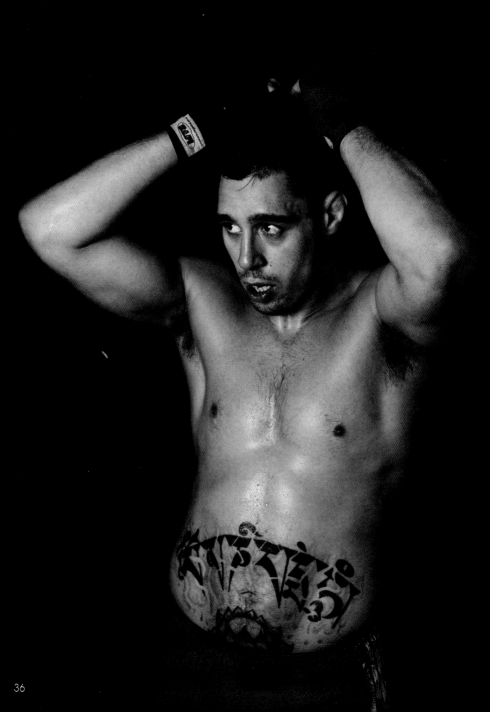

Robert Drysdale

Fabio Ferrari

41

Brad Pickett

'Old Skool' Neil Wain has just warmed up ahead of his fight with Rob Broughton at the ZT Heavyweight Tournament.

At 5' 10" and 250lbs, he has a speed that belies his size, something many of his opponents will attest to, having felt the power of his left hook first-hand.

Born:	May 9th, 1979
Nationality:	American
Height:	5' 8"
Weight:	155lbs
Division:	Lightweight
Nickname:	The Bully

The Bully is a perfect nickname for Gray Maynard, but not because of a need to psychologically terrorize his opponents; he garnered the nickname because of his unrelenting ability to control the flow of a fight and overcome opponents through strength, positioning and control – bullying his opponents into defeat.

Having faced his biggest challenge to date in Kenny Florian – a top-ten-ranked fighter by anyone's standard – Maynard is emerging as the next contender to square off with Frankie Edgar, the current UFC Lightweight champion.

Things are looking bright for this product of the Las Vegas-based Xtreme Couture stable.

46

Dmitry Samoilov / Bryan Harper

Ross Pointon

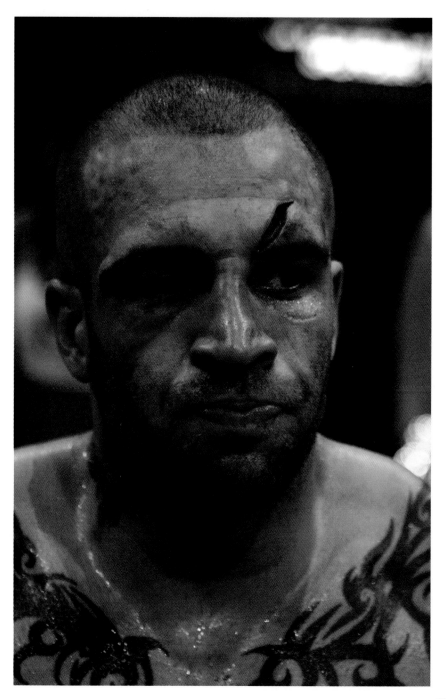

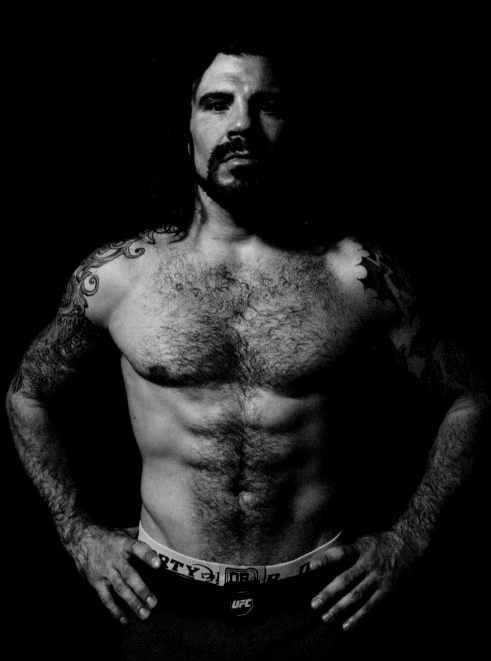

Born:	December 8th, 1981
Nationality:	American
Height:	5' 7"
Weight:	155lbs
Division:	Lightweight
Nickname:	The Carpenter

Clay Guida is a fighter's fighter, someone that comes to leave it all in the cage, not to pick up wins solely by registering a safe decision, not to avoid getting hit, not to play it safe until a submission appears. Guida likes to get in your face and push the pace.

On occasion this hyper level of activity has proven to be his downfall, but it guarantees his place in the promotion and his standing with the fans. You always know that when Guida is on the card there will be blood, there will be excitement and both fighters will come out of the encounter lumped up.

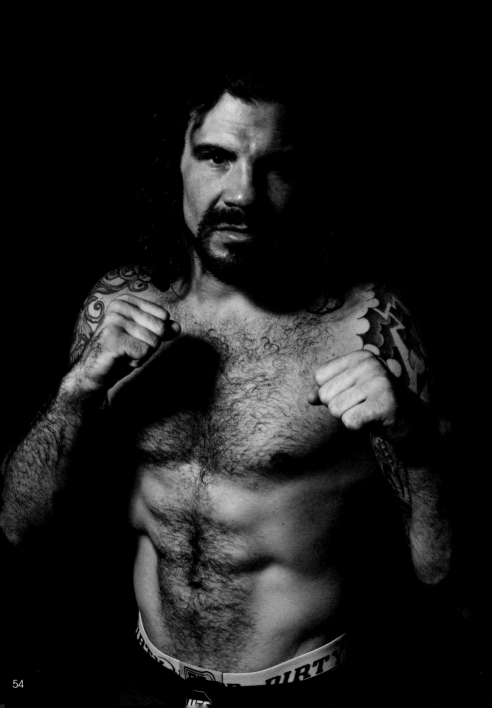

Edgelson Lua / John Maguire

Alan-Packman

56

Nick Chapman / Andrius Juska

Lola Bamgbala / Jack Mason

Born:	December 16th, 1978
Nationality:	English
Height:	6' 4"
Weight:	265lbs
Division:	Heavyweight
Nickname:	The Colossus / The Megapunk

A former bouncer and bodybuilder, James Thompson is famous for his intense staredowns, followed by the 'gong and dash' opening salvo he is so fond of doing in Japan.

Not exactly a shy individual, Thomspon is always willing to fight, anywhere, anytime. In some instances this approach has been detrimental to his record, but his refusal to back out of a challenge has made him a fan favourite.

JAMES THOMPSON

Marius Žaromskis suffered more than a loss in his encounter with Che Mills – he had to undergo delicate surgery for a torn tear duct below his right eye.

Whilst Ken Shamrock may have been one of my early MMA heroes, the highlight of my early reporting experience was talking to and training with Royce Gracie at Capital Jiu-Jitsu in Washington.

He proved to be every bit as eloquent about the Brazilian art as you would expect, but less so when discussing his loss to Matt Hughes.

The 'Whizzer' is one of my favourite moves to hit in sparring and I am still surprised that more fighters don't incorporate this into their arsenal when working the clinch and overhooks.

In this shot British Featherweight Ashleigh Grimshaw shows us how it's done with Paul Reed on the other end along for the ride.

Born:	March 18th, 1983
Nationality:	American
Height:	6' 4"
Weight:	265lbs
Division:	Heavyweight
Nickname:	The Hybrid

Brendan Schaub was all smiles after his appearance on *The Ultimate Fighter* reality TV show.

The Heavyweight prospect had been working hard with his camp in preparation for the Chase Gormley fight, but was content to take time out so that I could take some shots.

The former professional American football player is one of the few athletes to cross over from another sport to Mixed Martial Arts with huge success – namely six wins courtesy of strikes, all of which were within the first stanza.

w.angrrr

www.ca

Oli Thompson

Wayne Buck / Matteo Minonzio

74

Azran Quasid

Ian Butlin / Andy Butlin

Cut-men are a fascinating breed, and quite rare on the small-show MMA circuit, but their expertise in patching up fighters so they can continue in a bout is unmatched. Usually from a Martial Arts background themselves, cut-men understand how the skin reacts during trauma and can stop bleeding in its tracks.

In this shot, the UK's best cut-man Paul Marchant stems the flow of blood from Ross Mason's brow. What 'Paule' doesn't know about cuts isn't worth knowing.

He's a legend on the domestic circuit.

Born:	April 26th, 1984
Nationality:	American
Height:	6′ 2″
Weight:	170lbs
Division:	Welterweight
Nickname:	Natural Born Killer

Carlos Condit is a very experienced and wily fighter who has fought all over the world – from Hawaii to Japan, America, England, Canada and even Mexico. He is the former World Extreme Cagefighting Welterweight champion.

More recently, the UFC signee has been campaigning in the division with his eyes on the gold. Training out of the highly regarded Jackson's MMA camp, he is continually evolving as a fighter and it shows with the new tools he brings to each fight.

Tengiz Tedoradze

The time at the end of a fight spent waiting for a decision to be announced can seem like an eternity; you wonder if you have done enough, if the judges noticed everything you did during the bout – the submission attempts, ring control, effective aggression, strikes landed – and pray that they are fair in their judgement.

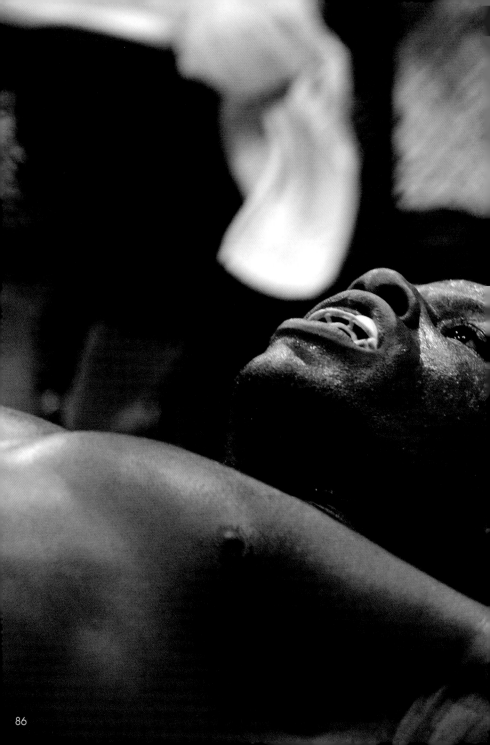

Earl Brown

Born:	February 13th, 1976
Nationality:	American
Height:	6' 1"
Weight:	185lbs
Division:	Middleweight
Nickname:	The Boogeyman

Dean Lister is one of the best pure submission wrestlers ever to compete in MMA but the results haven't been as forthcoming as in his grappling endeavours – time spent in the UFC and PRIDE organizations have showcased his chops on the deck, but his domination of the Abu Dhabi absolute division was a thing of legend.

Lister is a complete obsessive when it comes to the submission game, and is able to communicate with the BJJ players he spars with on account of being fluent in the language (he actually speaks four).

DEAN LISTER

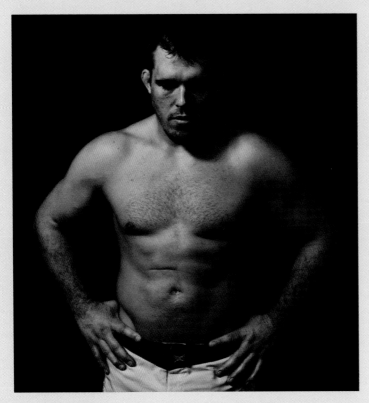

Tom Watson

93

The main concern after a big KO is the fighter's health, and that's why there is never a rush to remove them from the cage. Head trauma is a very real risk given the small amount of padding available in the gloves – 4oz to be precise.

Cliff Hall came out of his M-1 Challenge encounter with Christian Smith with nothing more than a sore head and a dent in his pride ... once he returned to consciousness.

A spinning backfist is quite a rare occurrence in MMA, quite often a flashy move that is invariably a miss rather than landing flush, but there are occasions where it lands on the button and the results are brutally effective – making it a move worth the risk.

Carl Noon

Born:	October 17th, 1975
Nationality:	American
Height:	6' 0"
Weight:	185lbs
Division:	Middleweight
Nickname:	Smokin' Joe

Joey Villaseñor is a hardened striker, having honed his craft on the job against some seriously tough opposition.

Having spent many years on the scene being extremely active, he is now balancing a fighting career with his position of striking coach at the Jackson's MMA Academy.

INTENSE FIGHTING

Roman Webber

Paul Cahoon / Earl Brown

Born:	July 29th, 1976
Nationality:	American
Height:	6' 0"
Weight:	170lbs
Division:	Welterweight
Nickname:	The Thoroughbred

Jay Hieron is one of the most successful fighters to rise out of the ashes of the now defunct IFL promotion. When the promotion folded he was the Welterweight champion and one of the hottest free agent commodities in the sport at the time.

Fast forward to present day and Hieron is once again a free agent having extricated himself from his Strikeforce contract. A place within the UFC beckons, adding further depth to an already stacked talent pool.

John Joe Ellis

Paul McVeigh

Damien Riccio struggles with his withdrawal from the bout with Michael Johnson.

Riccio has been in some wars on the domestic circuit over the years and his toughness is without question. He knows that a shattered nose isn't going to do him any favours and he risks further more complicated injuries if he continues.

Simeon Thoresen

Although not brothers in any genetic sense, Jimmy Wallhead (left) and Dan Hardy (right) are brothers by blood – blood they shed in training for the toughest physical encounters of their lives.

The sport of Mixed Martial Arts is one that creates a huge, lasting bond; you share the highs and lows of your team as if they were your own individual experiences. Everyone has your back – you sweat, batter and bleed with each other. This is your second family.

Beau King

Born:	November 24th, 1983
Nationality:	English
Height:	5' 9"
Weight:	170lbs
Division:	Welterweight
Nickname:	Scano

Yet another explosive talent to come out of the Liverpool-based Kaobon gym, Mark Scanlon holds an impressive record littered with first round stoppages – including a ten-second highlight-reel head kick knockout.

At 5' 9" and carrying a downtime weight of 200lbs, this recent UFC signee has a lot of power in his frame and, given the quality of talent he trains with in camp, is fast emerging as a big prospect for the future.

MARK SCANLON

Jay Hieron / John Alessio

Dan Henderson / Dean Lister

Jimmy Wallhead / Steven Lynch

Joe Vedepo / Oli Thompson

124

Colm Gillane / David Johnson

John Maguire / Simeon Thoresen

Born:	April 27th, 1987
Nationality:	American
Height:	6' 2"
Weight:	265lbs
Division:	Heavyweight
Nickname:	The Viking

Justin Wren made a splash on tenth season of *The Ultimate Fighter* TV show by defeating Wes Simms with an arm-triangle and looked to be one of the favourites for overall victory. Adding further weight to the long-running debate about judging criteria in MMA, Wren dropped from contention in the eliminator bout with eventual winner Roy Nelson.

Now fighting outside of the UFC and still picking up victories, Wren is still young enough and determined to make his way back into the mix. Training out of the Colorado-based Grudge facility weighs heavily in his favour, especially as so many bigger guys gravitate toward the camp.

JUSTIN WREN

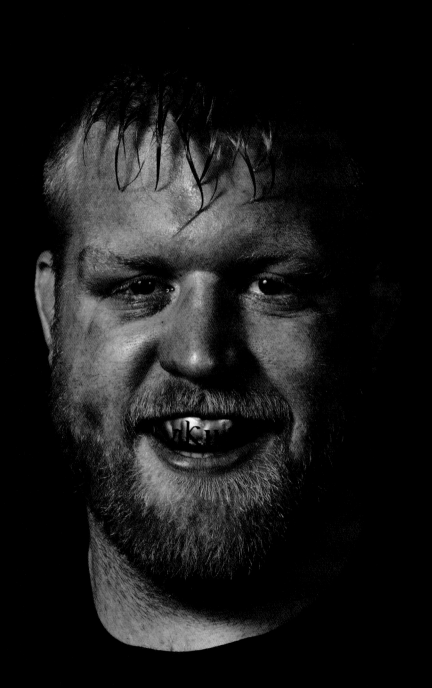

Marc Goddard watches on intently as Ashley Smith (right) attempts to decapitate
Aaron Blackwell (left)with a high kick.

Their bout would run the full fifteen minute duration, covering everything from strikes,
wrestling, takedowns and submission attempts, with Blackwell getting the eventual nod.

What this shot suggests to me is that Goddard's relaxed stance, yet focused eyes,
indicate he knew the strike wasn't going to stop the bout.

Jake Bostwick / John Maguire

Born:	December 6th, 1985
Nationality:	American
Height:	6′ 3″
Weight:	260lbs
Division:	Heavyweight
Nickname:	N/A

Considering he owns the UFC record for the fastest ever knockout at a mere seven seconds, it may surprise you to know that this fighter is no longer part of the promotion, having been released unexpectedly in September 2010.

Duffee has an incredible amount of potential but appears to have been blighted by injuries and match-making alterations that have, for one reason or another, kept him off fight cards.

He now faces a rebuilding of sorts in order to work his way back into the heavyweight division.

TODD DUFFEE

Paul Daley could hardly contain himself following his knockout victory over highly ranked European prospect Daniel Weichel to retain his World FX3 Welterweight title.

Frank Mir

Paul Ivens

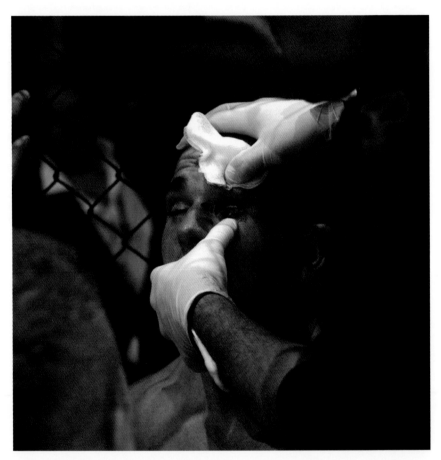

Most people have an aversion to looking at an eye injury, but if your job is to ensure the health of a fighter after a nasty cut or poke then you really have little choice in the matter.

In this shot an unintentional eye-poke by John Hathaway led to a nasty couple of weeks for the recovering Jack Mason. Fighters are used to dealing with broken bones, ligament strains and cuts, but an eye injury can prove particularly irritating and frustrating.

An overjoyed Przemyslaw Mysiala celebrated winning the UWC Light Heavyweight title by embracing his young son, who found the whole experience a little more upsetting!

A mix of emotions runs through the proud father – his son is the apple of his eye. Having lost a child during an earlier pregnancy, all he wants to do now is provide the best for his future and ensure he is safe.

144

Born:	May 24th, 1979
Nationality:	American
Height:	6'3"
Weight:	252lbs
Division:	Heavyweight
Nickname:	N/A

Frank Mir is one of those love/hate-type fighters, but there is no denying his abilities and desire to fight. In fact, Mir fought a much harder bout outside the cage when he tried to bounce back from a motorcycle accident that left him with some horrific injuries.

His initial post-accident performances depicted the fighter as a shadow of his former self, but through diligence, hard work and desire he eventually captured the UFC Interim Heavyweight Championship.

FRANK MIR

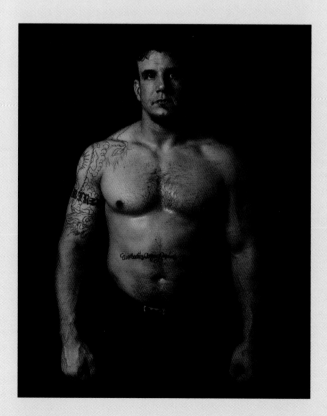

148

Dean Amasinger / Jason Muldoon

Head kick's always present a certain amount of risk and should be thrown with caution; all it takes is for your opponent to catch the leg and you're being taken down to the mat – hard.

Born:	February 27th, 1975
Nationality:	English
Height:	6' 1"
Weight:	244lbs
Division:	Heavyweight
Nickname:	N/A

Potter is a former professional boxer who has made the switch over to Mixed Martial Arts and now trains out of the Team Titan gym in North London under Mickey Papas.

Famous for his encounter with former British Boxing titleholder Danny Williams, Potter is a tough, heavy-handed fighter who is working diligently on his ground game. Impressions from his first fight are good, and, despite a disqualification, he exhibited some of the heaviest hands in the domestic division.

Daijirou Matsui

Jess Liaudin

Tom Watson / Sonny Dholakia

To win a championship is a huge achievement; to win two for your performances in the same night is something altogether. Marius Žaromskis came into the Dream Welterweight Grand Prix tournament as a highly touted European prospect, but wasn't expected to make it out of his first matchup with local fighter Seichi Ikemoto. A decision and two career highlight-reel knockouts later and he became the promotion's undisputed champion.

The promotion is based in Tokyo, Japan; its belts live in London, England.

Jimmy Wallhead / Dan Hardy

Linton Vassell

Born: January 2nd, 1983
Nationality: American
Height: 6' 1"
Weight: 185lbs
Division: Middleweight
Nickname: JT Money

Jessie Taylor will always be dogged by his appearance and subsequent dismissal from *The Ultimate Fighter* TV show. It's an unfortunate reality, but what it fails to portray is his solid wrestling base and his suffocating style.

Training out of Dan Henderson's Team Quest Murrieta facility, Taylor has been part of a camp that plays to his strengths and is trying to develop a post-UFC career, so much so that he went on a seven-fight win streak after departing from the promotion.

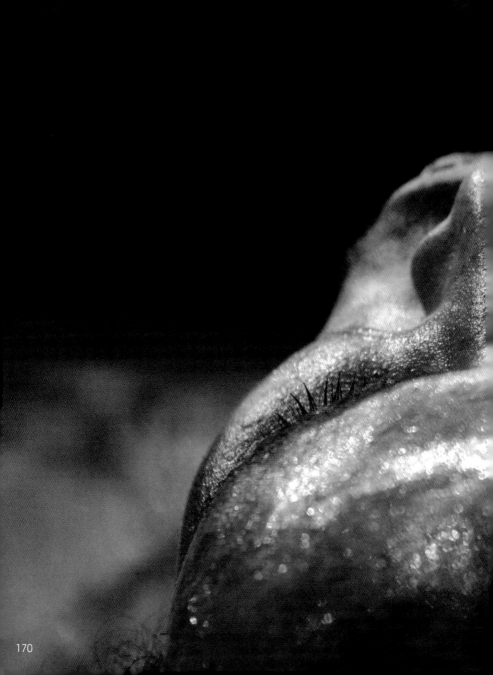

Jake Bostwick

Submissions are a devastating element of a fighter's arsenal: once on, a submission can cause anything from sleep to broken limbs and agonizing pain. Curiously, there are times when you think you are safe in a submission, but all it takes is a little tweak from your opponent to send waves of pain flooding through your system.

Born: August 27th, 1982
Nationality: American
Height: 5' 10"
Weight: 155lbs
Division: Lightweight
Nickname: The Lion

Ryan Couture hopes to forge his own career in MMA, not because of any expectation of following in his illustrious father's footsteps, but for his own personal satisfaction.

He has goals he wants to achieve, and, despite being at the helm of the family business, he still manages to hit the mats for the pro training sessions.

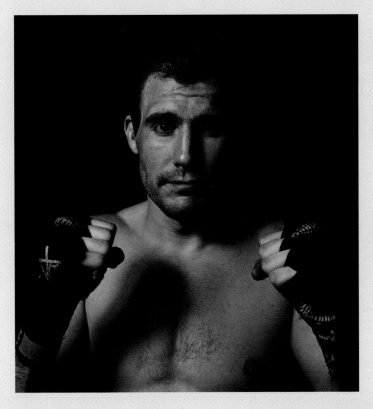

Henrique Santana / Yasubey Enomoto

Alex Reid

Brad Pickett

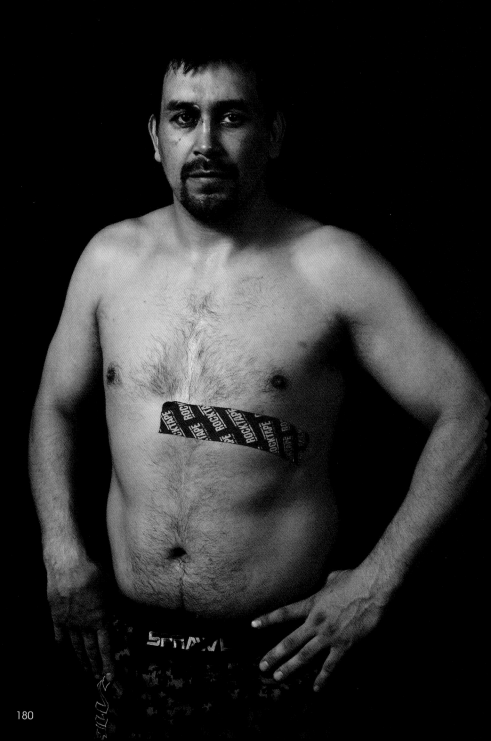

Born:	January 16th, 1974
Nationality:	American
Height:	6' 2"
Weight:	246lbs
Division:	Heavyweight
Nickname:	The Headhunter

Paul Buentello is one of the true veterans of Mixed Martial Arts in America, and yet he didn't fight in the early UFCs and he isn't known for being a campaigner of a particular style of Martial Arts. Buentello is a veteran because he represents the kind of fighter that fought his way through the early MMA scene and ascended through the ranks to become top-flight talent.

He is a veteran of many wars and the look in his eyes reflects this.

John Kelly / Keith Singh

Danielle West / Willemijn Van Zon

Born: August 4th, 1988
Nationality: English
Height: 6' 1"
Weight: 155lbs
Division: Lightweight
Nickname: Sassangle

Earning your nickname because you have been able to submit
seven consecutive opponents with the same triangle submission is
a somewhat dubious honour. Irrespective, this highly regarded fighter
is proving to be a danger in all elements of the game.

Proving true to his moniker, Paul Sass made a successful UFC debut
by submitting Mark Holst – picking up 'Sub of the Night' honours
as well.

Carlos Condit

189

Ian Freeman / Paul Cahoon

Tom Watson

Nottingham-based former boxer Wayne Buck works his ground-and-pound offence, cutting a shape that reminds me of the old Greek Olympics. Combat sports are nothing new in the history of man, but the earliest form of combat with a resemblance to Mixed Martial Arts was called Pankration and dates to 648 bc, when it was introduced into the Olympics.

Born:	July 30th, 1980
Nationality:	Lithuanian
Height:	5' 9"
Weight:	170lbs
Division:	Welterweight
Nickname:	The Whitemare

Marius Žaromskis made his pro MMA debut back in his Lithuanian homeland before coming the UK for work. His calling as a martial artist prevailed though and it wasn't long before he was carving a path on the domestic scene, blasting through a collection of tough fighters with his explosive striking style.

Japan came calling in April 2009, when he was offered a slot in the Dream Welterweight Grand Prix tournament. Not expected to do well by many, Žaromskis notched a unanimous decision in his debut before nearly decapitating two highly regarded fighters, and picked up the dual titles in the promotion.

Subsequent explorations in the American-based Strikeforce promotion haven't been as agreeable for the fighter, but a return to his stomping ground in Japan appears to be his main focus for the future.

MARIUS ŽAROMSKIS

Paul Daley

Scott Jansen / Azran Quasid

Fighting with an open mouth and a barbell tongue piercing is just plain dangerous ... but it wasn't until the end of the second round that referee Marc Goddard found this out – by which point it was too late to do anything about it.

Fabricio Nascimento had his jaw tested several times in his bout with Jim Wallhead and thankfully escaped major injury, but the risks of entanglement, choking on the piercing and tearing of the tongue, make his an inadvisable MMA accessory. Leaving your mouth open during a fight is inviting disaster – your jaw will have enough movement to either become dislodged or slide back into the nerves behind it, leaving you either broken or an unconscious mess on the floor.

Born: September 8th, 1982
Nationality: Polish
Height: 6' 1"
Weight: 205lbs
Division: Light Heavyweight & Heavyweight
Nickname: Misiek

This Polish-born fighter is consistently ranked in the UK as one of the top prospects at Light Heavyweight and has even competed as a Heavyweight in the past.

Originally hitting the scene as a submission fighter, courtesy of a solid grounding in BJJ at Ze Marcello's Brazilian Top Team, he has since transferred camps to London Shootfighters and rounded out his striking and wrestling.

Elvis Sinosec / Paul Cahoon

Elvis Sinosec

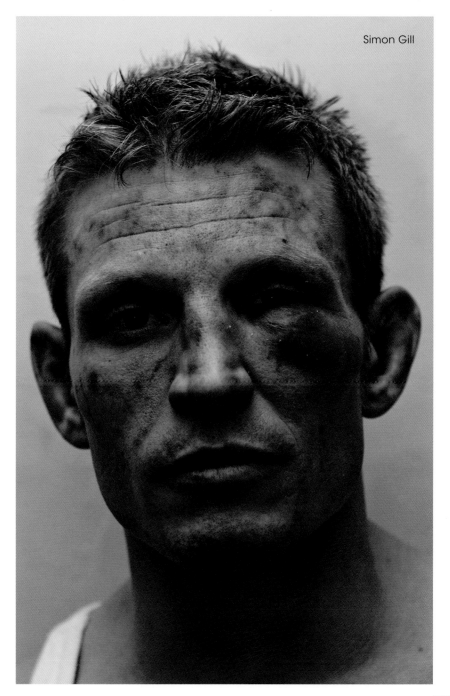

Simon Gill

Born:	August 24th, 1970
Nationality:	American
Height:	5' 11"
Weight:	185lbs & 205lbs
Division:	Middleweight & Light Heavyweight
Nickname:	Hendo

There aren't many fighters out there who have achieved as much as Dan Henderson has, from being a former Olympian wrestler to becoming a dual title holder within the PRIDE organization.

He has always strived to achieve more from himself and the sport and has never been embroiled in the typical verbal spats and hyperbole that current fighters seem to be so fond of.

Even from his earlier days in Japan, fighting two weight classes outside of his natural classification, he still managed to pick up wins over top-flight competition.

As far as role models go, Henderson exemplifies the proverbial wisdom of Theodore Roosevelt: 'Speak softly and carry a big stick.'

Murillo 'Ninja' Rua gives his seal of approval following a successful return to action at Cage Rage 24.

Many detractors dismissed the promotion, having failed to appreciate truly what it was bringing to the sport at the time. International players were rebuilding their careers, new stars cut their teeth and there was an intermediary platform which benefited the UK MMA scene.

I never asked James Thompson if he remembers seeing me after being knocked out so brutally at the hands of Neil Grove, but I do know that he doesn't remember much about the fight other than what he has seen on video.

This often occurs with fighters who have been knocked out cold and many would much rather forget about the experience then recollect a loss.

Vaseline is usually applied to the bridge of the nose, the eyebrows and the top of the cheek bones.

It is primarily intended to allow strikes to land but reduce the risks of cuts. Some fighters have a lot of scar tissue build-up in the face and are prone to being stopped because of old injuries re-opening

A new trend in MMA for 'cutters' is to have the facial bones 'shaved'.

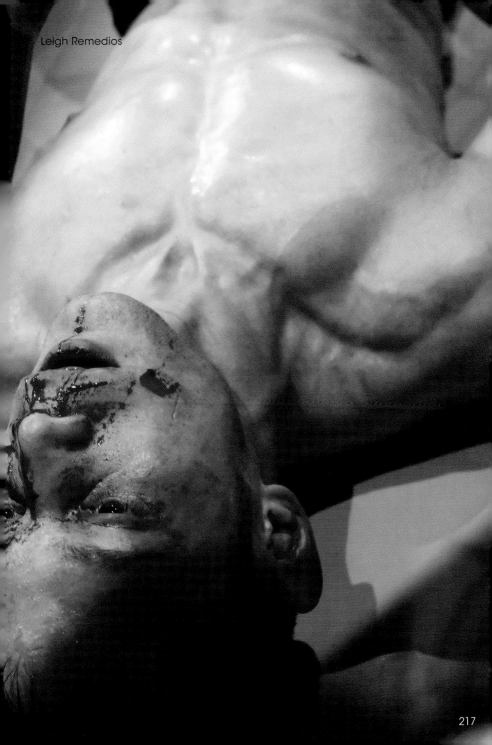

Leigh Remedios

217

Danny Batten

Born: September 26th, 1984
Nationality: English
Height: 5' 8"
Weight: 155lbs
Division: Lightweight
Nickname: The Real Deal

A crisp and natural striker, Pearson is an explosive commodity in the cage and is more than happy to mix it up on all levels – as evidenced by the submission wins that punctuate his record. He came to prominence through a series of impressive wins on *The Ultimate Fighter: United States vs United Kingdom* series that eventually resulted in him becoming the overall winner at Lightweight.

Always exciting, Pearson is a fearless fighter and throws hard – just check his 'Fight of the Night' clash with tough German Dennis Siver for reference. Many have tipped the Sunderland terror as a future champion; given his raw talent and athleticism, he may just prove them right.

ROSS PEARSON

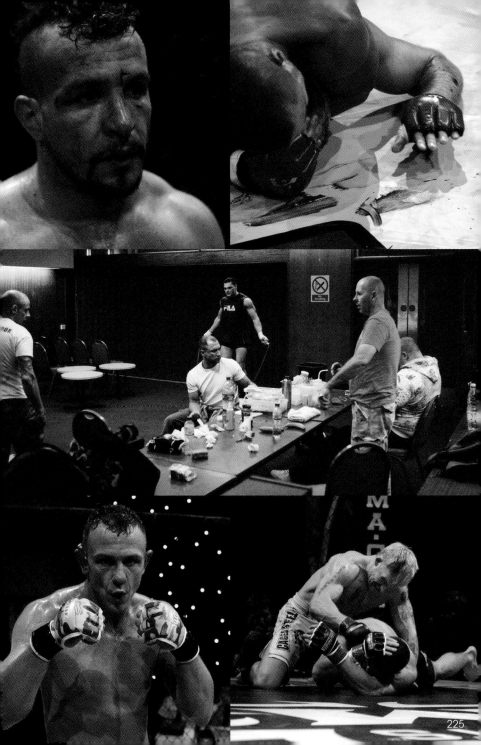

Born:	August 12th, 1982
Nationality:	English
Height:	5' 11"
Weight:	185lbs
Division:	Middleweight
Nickname:	The Stone

Jack Mason is a full-time financial project manager by day, holding down complex projects with huge responsibilities, but four times a year or so he steps out of the suit and into the cage to do battle as a Middleweight. He currently holds the CFC championship belt and is always looking to add new skills to his arsenal.

Training out of the Team Tsunami camp in Cambridge, Mason has always seen MMA as an outlet for his energy and a way to test himself away from his day job. There are few fighters on the circuit today who still manage to hold down a working week and fight at his level.

JACK MASON

Highly regarded Wolfslair BJJ instructor Mario 'Sukata' Neto is left to deal with the consequences of his submission loss at the hands of UFC-bound Stefan Struve.

For a Brazilian, being submitted in a fight isn't something that sits well, but it takes nothing away from his achievements as a coach for one the UK's most successful camps.

This is the face of a fighter who is done under the weight of a heavy-handed ground-and-pound assault, taken mere moments before the referee steps in to rescue him.

The human emotion that comes with getting pounded out can't be seen on the TV.

Paul Reed

Born:	February 21st, 1983
Nationality:	English
Height:	5' 9"
Weight:	170lbs
Division:	Welterweight
Nickname:	Semtex

Owner of possibly the heaviest hands at Welterweight in the UK, Paul Daley has had a career punctuated by controversy and brutal knockouts. His post-fight sucker-punch toward Josh Koscheck drew the ire of UFC president Dana White, who subsequently exiled him from the promotion; but 'Semtex' is used to paving his own way when it comes to fighting, adopting the ancient samurai philosophy of the Ronin – a warrior without master.

He now finds himself in the thick of the Strikeforce Welterweight picture, but still relishes the opportunity to accept new challenges and – born to battle – will fight anyone, anywhere.

PAUL DALEY

Armbar submissions come from many angles, as ably demonstrated by
Jim Burman (above) in his victorious encounter at UWC 11.

The submission itself can be devastating, but there are warnings before a break
occurs: the first is the pain of nerves being hyper-extended; the second is
a loud pop as nerves slide out of alignment with the bone.

Anything after that requires surgery.

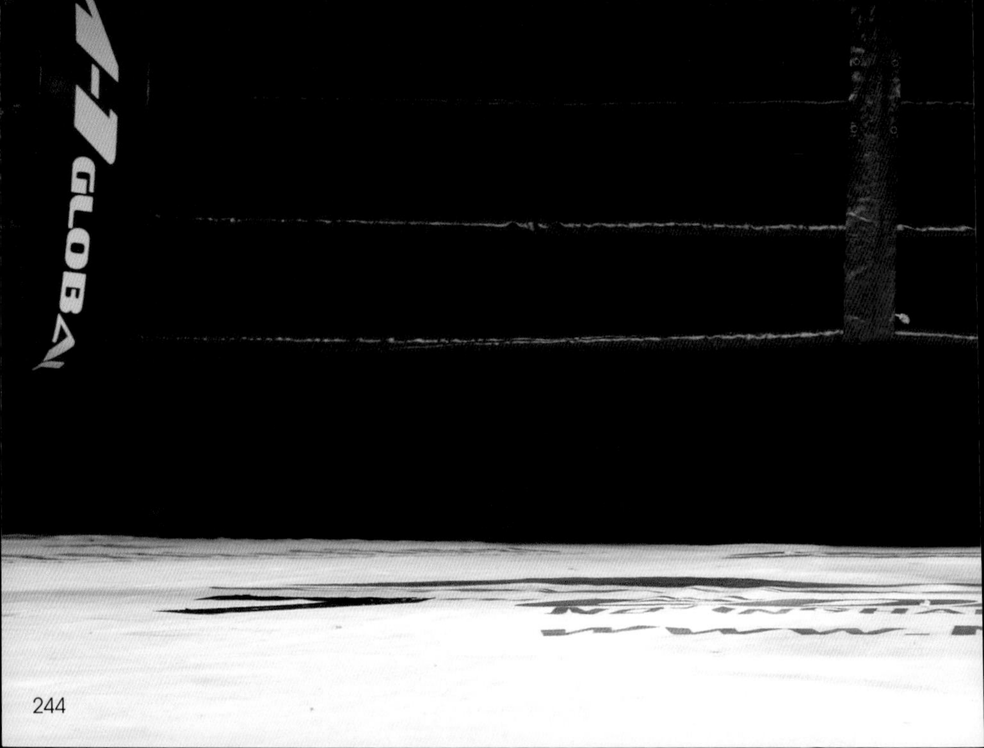

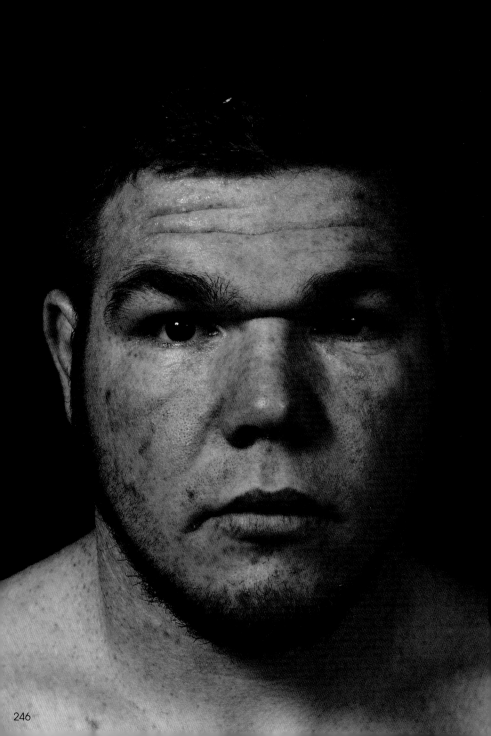

Born: December 10th, 1987
Nationality: British
Height: 5' 7"
Weight: 155lbs
Division: Lightweight
Nickname: 2 Gunz

Appearances can be deceiving and Tom Maguire is testament to that fact: he's a short, stocky individual who looks quite unassuming away from the cage – but put him in it and you see a very different animal indeed.

Fighting runs through the family lineage with the Maguire brothers, and both are key lynchpins in the Tsunami fight team.

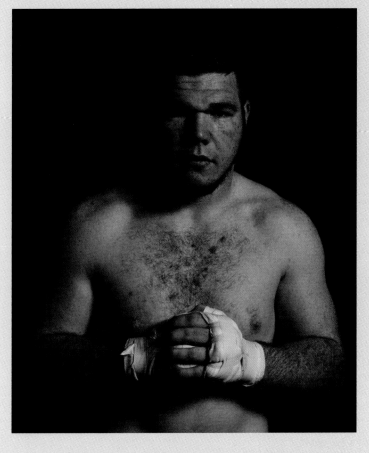

Liam Etebar / Colin French

249

Matt Horwich / Tom Watson

Stav Economou / Linton Vassell

Rob Broughton

251

Eric Esch

David Abbott

Born: June 20th, 1965
Nationality: American
Height: 6' 2"
Weight: 205lbs
Division: Light Heavyweight
Nickname: N/A

A highly decorated NCAA Division 1 wrestler in his own right, Van Arsdale made the transition to Mixed Martial Arts when he flew out to Brazil to compete in the International Vale Tudo championships, blasting through three native competitors in their own backyard.

Now officially retired from competition, he is one of the best wrestling coaches out there – evidenced as much through his work with Jackson's MMA and Grudge Sports as through his tenure on *The Ultimate Fighter* show. I loved his encounter with Randy Couture and it was a pleasure watching two high-level wrestlers engage like that in the Octagon.

MIKE VAN ARSDALE

Paul Daley

Joe Mac

Unencumbered by the bright lights, adrenaline dump and screaming of the crowd, your corner is continually assessing how your opponent is attacking, where their weaknesses are and what you can do to exploit them.

A smart corner will look at things from two angles: one will look at your opponent; the other will look at you. Between the two of them you should have a clear picture of what to do.

Everything moves so fast in a fight, but nothing's quicker than the sixty seconds between rounds.

Born:	March 14th, 1984
Nationality:	English
Height:	5' 10"
Weight:	170lbs
Division:	Welterweight
Nickname:	Judo

Jimmy Wallhead has often been overlooked on the international scene and was left to hone his skills on the domestic circuit, tightening his boxing and wrestling to a point where the 'Judo' part of his nickname is something of a misnomer.

Wallhead is now part of the Bellator Fighting Championships promotion and made a big splash on his debut by defeating Ryan Thomas – a welcome reward for years of hard work, persistence and sacrifice. It just goes to show that even in the bleakest of times, strength of will and determination can pull you through.

only God Can
Judge Me

James Thompson

Danny Batten

Vinnie Lopez

Popek Rak

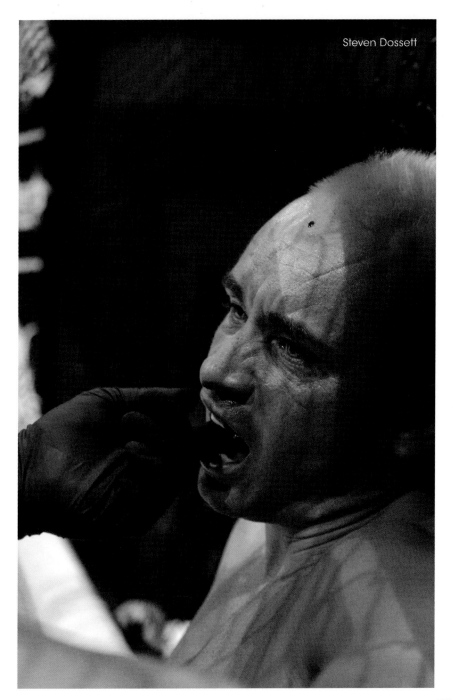

Steven Dossett

269

Born:	July 14th, 1979
Nationality:	Mexican American
Height:	5' 10"
Weight:	145lbs
Division:	Featherweight
Nickname:	Bad Boy

Human fireball Leonard Garcia burst onto the radar at UFC 69 in a spectacular fight with the highly regarded Roger Huerta, immediately making an impression for his balls-out style and sense of humour when getting hit in the face. Leonard fought a couple of times again at 155lbs before making the switch to the WEC and a more natural fighting weight of 145lbs.

Since then he has been known for his exciting style, fastball punches and slick Brazilian Jiu-Jitsu; furthermore, he is a straight-up guy outside of the cage with a good sense of humour.

LEONARD GARCIA

Kaobon Fight Team

275

Born:	July 23rd, 1987
Nationality:	English
Height:	6′ 2″
Weight:	170lbs
Division:	Welterweight
Nickname:	The Hitman

Hathaway is a product of hard work and single-minded determination, having started his career under the tutelage of close friend and mentor Sol Gilbert, before evolving to the London Shootfighters camp and into the UFC as a Welterweight contender.

His most notable win came as a huge surprise to many as he systematically dismantled former UFC title challenger Diego Sanchez over three rounds. Always one to remain grounded and humble, Hathaway is one of the most approachable fighters around and remains unchanged by the bright lights and cameras that now surround him.

JOHN HATHAWAY

Paul Cahoon

Born:	March 31st, 1900
Nationality:	English
Height:	6′ 2″
Weight:	185lbs
Division:	Middleweight
Nickname:	The Messenger

Despite being a very tough, technical boxer, James Zikic has a finesse on the ground that belies a man of his size.

An obsessive student of the sport, Zikic has taken himself off to places like Brazil over the years to hone his technical repertoire.

Mostly known for his war with Evangelista 'Cyborg' Santos and subsequent fight with Vitor Belfort, Zikic has always had a career punctuated by periods of inactivity, though usually manages to shake off ring rust through sheer determination and pure single mindedness.

The steely gaze you see opposite only hints at the mental toughness that lurks inside the man. Zikic believes in the divine and feels that nothing can take him away from his path in life.

JAMES ZIKIC

John Cornett / Mikhail Zayats

Ross Mason / Scott Jansen

James McSweeney

Born: February 18th, 1982
Nationality: English
Height: 5' 11"
Weight: 170lbs
Division: Welterweight

Michael Johnson has been fighting on the domestic scene for ten years, although you wouldn't know it because his record equates to roughly a fight per year;

This heavy-handed ground-and-pound specialist is looking finally to string together a consistent career, having moved camps, re-assessed his physical strategy and restored his interest in the sport of Mixed Martial Arts. A new member of the BAMMA roster, things are starting to look up for the veteran.

MICHAEL JOHNSON

Lewis Barrow / Jimmy Wallhead

Consolation from your opponent isn't what you step into the cage for, but if victory proves to be elusive at least you know that your opponent respects you. There are times when bad blood gets in the way of things, but in the main, win or lose, MMA fighters have a deep-seated respect for each other and can remain friends long after they fight.

Ian Freeman

Born:	July 13th, 1982
Nationality:	English
Height:	6' 0"
Weight:	185lbs
Division:	Middleweight
Nickname:	Kong

Having started his MMA training on a farm, it didn't take long for Watson to realize that he wanted to fight for a living, and in doing so took himself off to train in America at an early age. Since then he has moved around the United States and Canada, seeking out the best instruction on offer, drawing a close allegiance to Jackson's and Georges St-Pierre's camps along the way.

Famous in the UK for his exciting battles in the BAMMA promotion – including the long awaited clash with Alex Reid – Watson has always stayed true to his roots as a fighter's fighter.

Mark Weir / Mohammed Kacha

Tony Papas / Gaz Roriston

Daniel Thomas / Andre Winner

Fabricio Nascimento / Jimmy Wallhead

Born:	July 5th, 1979
Nationality:	Canadian
Height:	5' 9"
Weight:	170lbs
Division:	Welterweight
Nickname:	The Natural

John Alessio is a veteran Canadian fighter despite being still quite young; he has competed in all of the Mixed Martial Arts promotions of note, including spells in the UFC, PRIDE, WEC, Dream, KOTC and MFC and is now part of the Bellator roster.

He is a very versatile athlete who is always game at any stage of a fight. Now training out of the Xtreme Couture camp in Las Vegas, Alessio is still going strong despite having had over forty fights and shows no sign of slowing down.

Earl Brown

Holly Holm

Tarec Saffiedine

Tapping when one arm is in danger and the other is wedged under your opponent's leg is always going to be difficult; in this instance you have to rely on the person submitting you to relinquish when you tap them gently on the feet with your fingers.

Thankfully for Mark O'Toole, he had one such opponent in Matt Thorpe.

Born:	December 15th, 1979
Nationality:	English
Height:	6' 0"
Weight:	155lbs
Division:	Lightweight
Nickname:	Relentless

Taylor made his UFC Welterweight debut in Manchester, opening fans' eyes with his relentless assault on Brazilian export Edilberto de Oliveira, but has since had a mixed batch of results that, on paper, don't do his performances justice – he has been one half of a 'Fight of the Night' bonus on three separate occasions.

Recently dropping to a more natural weight class of 155lbs and retooling himself with the famed Liverpool-based Team Kaobon, Taylor is looking to the future and hoping to string together a consistent set of results in the promotion.

PAUL TAYLOR

Dean Amasinger

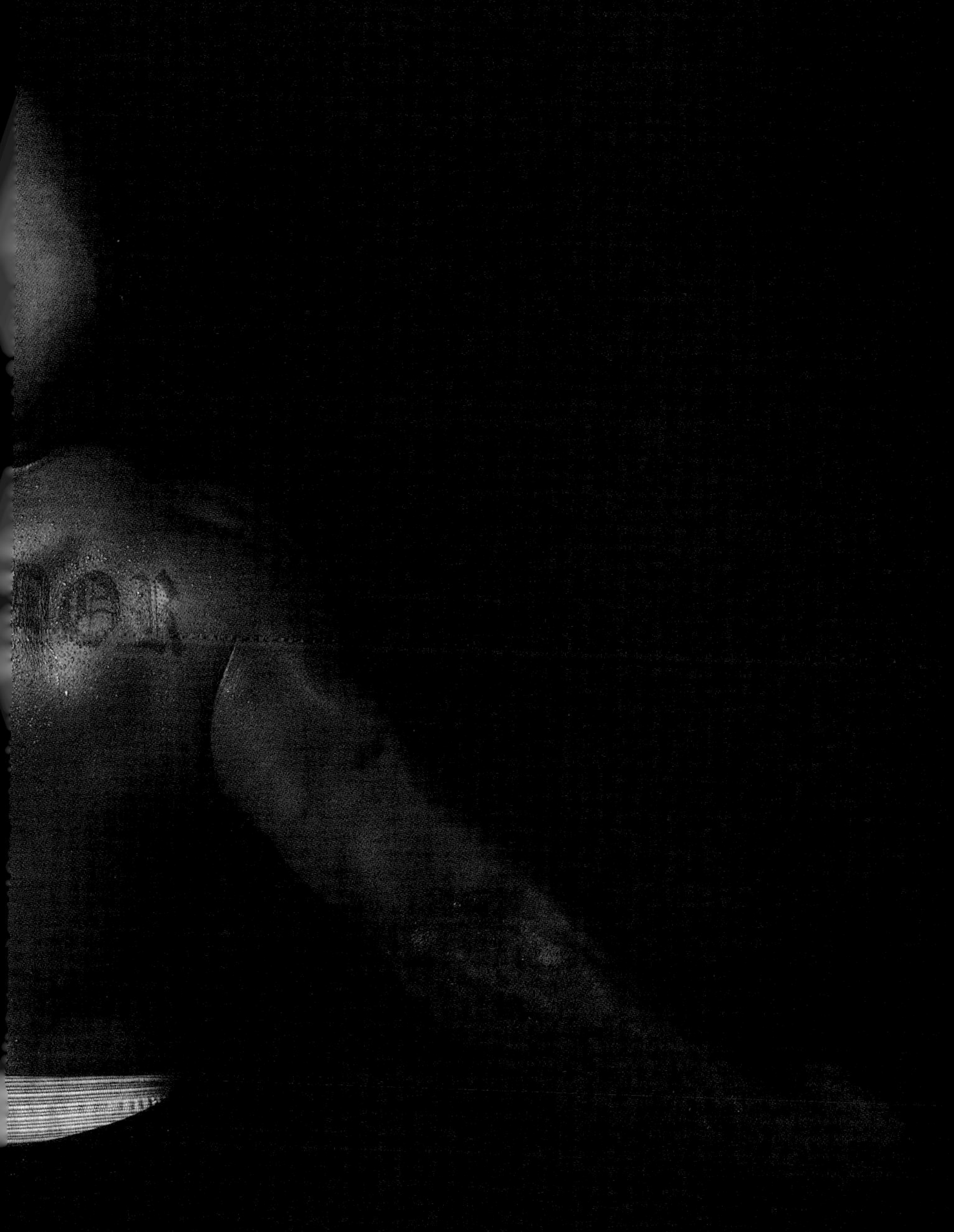

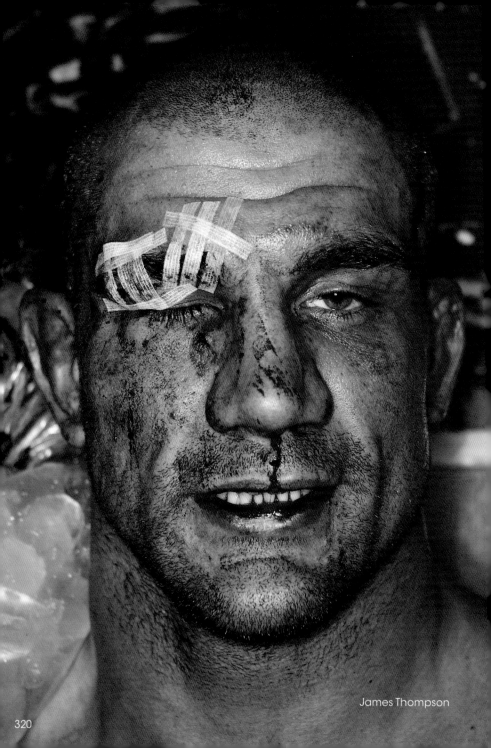

James Thompson

Top world-ranked Lightweight fighter Vitor 'Shaolin' Ribiero applies a straight armbar from the bottom, forcing Diasuke Nakamura to tap. Unfortunately, by this point, Nakamura had already suffered a three-point fracture to his arm.

Knockouts are visually brutal. Submissions are brutal on a whole other level.

Francis Heagney

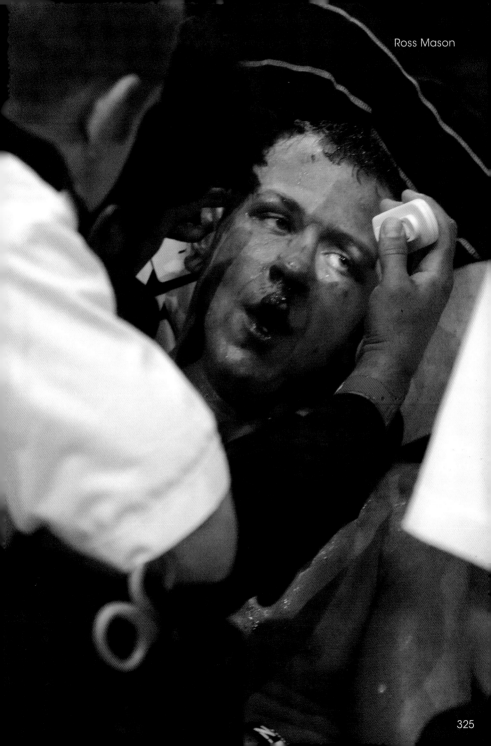

Ross Mason

325

Born: April 2nd, 1984
Nationality: English
Height: 5' 11"
Weight: 170lbs
Division: Welterweight
Nickname: N/A

Lewis is a highly touted prospect who has a wealth of experience as a semi-pro but remains relatively untested in professional bouts. He has a background in Martial Arts that spans nearly twenty years of striking arts and it shows in the speed and intensity of his attack.

No one likes to be choked out – it is one of the most claustrophobic, terrifying feelings; but to get through it you need to be relaxed and follow a precise series of movements for escape – if you don't you either 'tap out' or pass out ...

What's the best way to avoid this scenario? Never give your opponent your back!

Brad Wheeler (right) eats a big fist from Dino Gambatesa (left) on his way down to the mat.

Forty seconds, over and out.

Born:	March 19th, 1984
Nationality:	English
Height:	5' 9"
Weight:	170lbs
Division:	Welterweight
Nickname:	The Renegade

Dean Amasinger was starting to make waves before hitting
The Ultimate Fighter show through impressive performances in the
FX3 and Cage Warriors promotions. An understudy of Paul Daley in
the Rough House team, Amasinger bounced back from a loss on the
show with two consecutive victories before suffering an ulna break
when vying for the Ultimate Challenge Welterweight title.

A very analytical fighter and a good corner man, Amasinger
combines his studious approach to the game with a powerhouse
physique to achieve results. The toughest fight he has had so far has
been the battle back to the cage from injury.

Amar Suloev

Born: August 4th, 1978
Nationality: American
Height: 6' 0"
Weight: 170lbs
Division: Welterweight
Nickname: Bang

Horrific injuries can sometimes occur in MMA, most of them by accident rather than design. 'Bang' Ludwig fell foul of one such injury during his encounter with Darren Elkins.

Looking to stuff a takedown attempt, he suffered a Maisonneuve fracture that will put him out of action for six months and leave him with two permanent steel pins in his ankle.

The road to recovery for any fighter is a hard one to navigate, if you consider that fighters' whole lives evolve around being active and really pushing their bodies to the limit; you start to wonder about how they cope with the frustrations of being unable to train.

John Maguire / Edgelson Lua

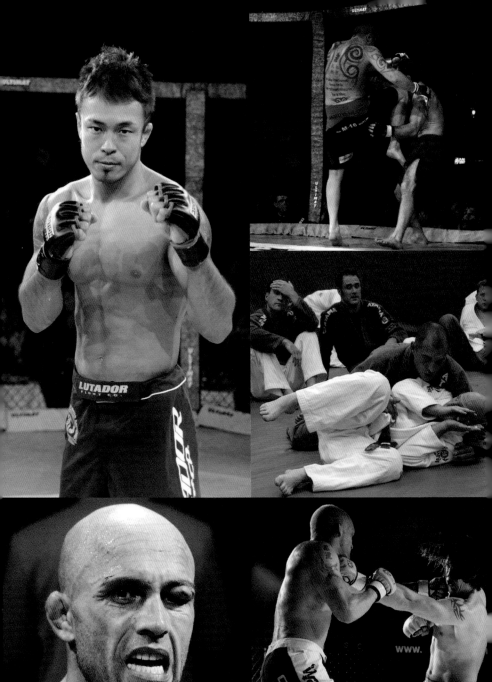

342

Born:	April 1st, 1977
Nationality:	Brazilian
Height:	6′ 0″
Weight:	185lbs
Division:	Middleweight
Nickname:	The Phenom

Brazilian Vitor Belfort is a complex man, famously inconsistent and enigmatic, but when his head is in the game he is world class; when it's not, he is everything but.

I managed to catch up with him on the eve of his encounter with Ivan Serati at Cage Rage and was given an insight into a man who has faced more adversity than most – steroid suspension; revolving-door training camps; rejection; the emotional rollercoaster of winning and losing the UFC Light Heavyweight Championship.

Belfort has conquered his demons and come to terms with his past. True warriors face adversity and come out the other side whole.

The proof of this acceptance his been evident in the results, as he has blasted his way through opponents, appearing for all this world like the 'Old Vitor' en route to a title shot in the UFC against one of the pound-for-pound best: Anderson Silva.

James Zikic

Tom Blackledge

347

Rob Sinclair

Born:	April 26th, 1965
Nationality:	American
Height:	6' 0"
Weight:	265lbs
Division:	Heavyweight
Nickname:	Tank

'Tank' Abbott is a fighter who made a massive impact in the UFC during the early years, but one who is unlikely ever to be inducted into the promotion's Hall of Fame.

He is a man who has spent a lifetime fighting and will be happy to continue doing so as the years pass, but maybe not under the vigilant eye of TV cameras.

'Tank' is a reminder of days gone by. His mean, street-fighting approach came as a breath of fresh air at a time when traditional martial arts were favoured, and changed people's perceptions of what 'tough' actually meant.

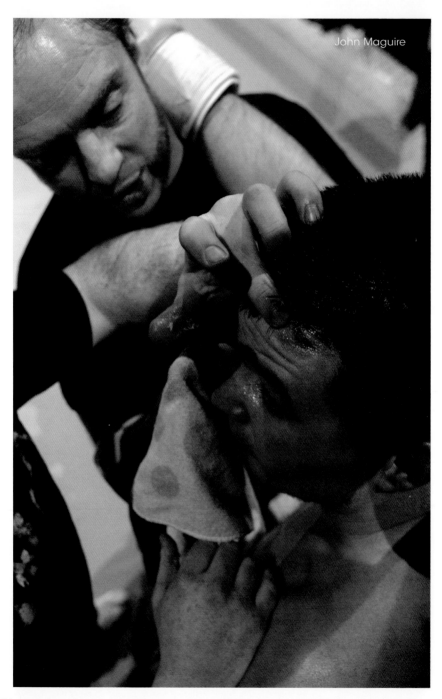

John Maguire

Ivan Serati

Born: January 11th, 1986
Nationality: English
Height: 6' 1"
Weight: 155lbs
Division: Lightweight
Nickname: N/A

Terry Etim is a hidden gem in the UFC Lightweight division at the moment. A completely fluid mix of Muay Thai and Luta Livre, but somehow, aside from the support of hardcore fans, he remains relatively under-exposed in the grand scheme of things.

He was the spearhead fighter for the Kaobon gym, paving the way and drawing eyes to the now highly vaunted squad. He is tall, rangy and part of the new breed of fighters that will carry the sport beyond the current veterans.

John Cornett

Sami Berik / Mark Smith

Leon Roberts

Martin Stapleton / David Johnson

Born: July 17th, 1984
Nationality: English
Height: 5' 10"
Weight: 155lbs
Division: Lightweight
Nickname: Who Where

Skill wise, Wenn is one of the most complete fighters to come out of the Tsunami camp. His arsenal is a slick mix of submissions and strikes coupled with a durability that comes only from a deep-seated desire to fight – evident in several wars he has been involved in during his career. Unfortunately, inconsistency has been the biggest negative skewed against him.

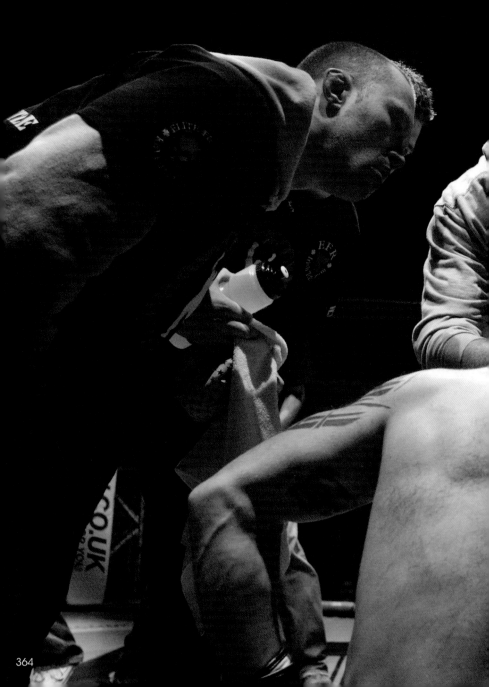

Aiden Marron

TIMAT

Matteo Piran

Born: February 14th, 1986
Nationality: English / Angolan
Height: 5' 10"
Weight: 170lbs
Division: Welterweight
Nickname: Edge

Originally from a Karate background, this fighter has augmented his training through the incorporation of Brazilian Jiu-Jitsu and Muay Thai and has become a staple on the London fight circuit due to his tenacity and the diversity of his arsenal.

Ross Mason / Ross Pointon

Paul Daley

Early UK MMA trailblazer Lee Hasdell reflects on his disappointing return to competition in 2007. Injuries heal, but pride takes much longer to mend itself.

Lifetime martial artists always have a hard time finding their place when the curtain comes down on their fighting career. Some walk away altogether, but Hasdell is now much more involved in the sport outside of the cage.

Born:	July 19th, 1987
Nationality:	American
Height:	6' 4"
Weight:	205lbs
Division:	Light Heavyweight
Nickname:	Bones

Jon Jones – the future of the UFC Light Heavyweight division? Quite possibly – his obliteration of opponents through an unorthodox striking style and solid Greco wrestling background certainly give him the tools to become so.

Big things are expected of this explosive young fighter and so far he hasn't disappointed. Always willing to try something new and bring some exciting variations to the already patented way of fighting MMA, Jones is both creative and highly capable.

Mazakasu Imanari (top) is one of the most unique fighters on the planet – a pioneer of sorts in the art of Kamikaze Jiu-Jitsu.

In his bout with Robbie Olivier (bottom), he launched himself in the air with an attempted head stomp. Factoring gravity into the equation, he came down partially attached to Olivier's arm – who tried to extract himself from the chaos, creating all the pressure Imanari required to force the tap.

Even the most experienced of MMA commentators can still struggle to explain to the befuddled viewer exactly what is going on when someone like Imanari is working his magic.

Trevor Wittman

Born:	November 28th, 1978
Nationality:	Puerto Rican
Height:	6′ 0″
Weight:	185lbs
Division:	Middleweight
Nickname:	The Assault

Appearances can be deceiving, and that is exactly the case when it comes to Vinnie Lopez – a religious and loyal family man who steps into the cage to fight for his son and daughter.

Coming from a boxing background, Lopez is a serious stand-up fighter. He first encountered Mixed Martial Arts in 2003 though he only really started to get serious about it in 2008. Since that time he feels that it has given him the discipline and focus that were missing in his life and that it has made him a better person.

VINNIE LOPEZ

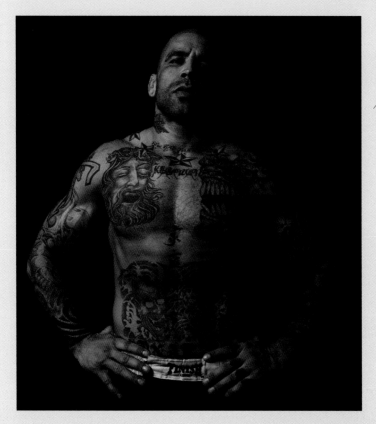

Mixed emotions register on Jean Silva's face (left) as he reluctantly snaps fellow Brazilian Danillo Cherman's arm above the elbow.

The bone-crunching armbar submission failed to yield victory as Cherman soldiered through another round and a half to pick up the unanimous decision victory.

Sometimes an opponent is so tough that you are forced to go to extremes, but that still doesn't always guarantee victory.

Matt Smith

Matteo Piran / Przemyslaw Mysiala

Born: June 29th, 1981
Nationality: American
Height: 6' 1"
Weight: 261lbs
Division: Heavyweight
Nickname: Iron Mike

For all his achievements inside the cage, Whitehead appears to have had some problems levelled at him outside of it. Unfortunately this takes away from the fact that he recently became the IFC Heavyweight Champion with a solid win over fellow UFC veteran Chase Gormley.

Whitehead is a tough, well-rounded and dangerous opponent at all levels of the game, and has been able to bounce effectively between Heavyweight and Light Heavyweight divisions. Having had his Strikeforce tenure cut short by controversy, this three-time All American Wrestler is now looking to rebuild his career – having a title is a good way to start.

The gym is a place where you learn new techniques, pressure test yourself, bleed and develop strategies – but it's much more than that. Many find that their closest friends are the people they train with and when that happens, the gym ceases to become a place of work: it becomes your second home.

Before a session starts, you will usually find pockets of guys hanging around, gassing about what they have been eating, things they've got up to and generally having a laugh with their friends about exploits outside of training.

Unlike many other sports, MMA is one of the closest-knit communities when it comes to camaraderie and friendship.

Evangelista Santos

Christian Smith

Mike Wessell

Born:	September 12th, 1984
Nationality:	English
Height:	5' 10"
Weight:	155lbs
Division:	Lightweight
Nickname:	Tellys

Paul Kelly is one of the nicest people you could meet in this game – he is staunchly loyal to his team, his family and his friends, and he never sugar-coats his views. Couple that with a massive competitive streak and you have a fighter who will go through hell to make those around him proud.

What a lot of people don't know about Kelly is that he suffered injuries at an early age which would have made a lesser person think twice about combative sports – his leg still bears the scars of an accident that left him with horrific burns and nerve damage. Through strength of character and a single-minded determination to succeed, Kelly was able to overcome his setbacks and push to the very edge of his physical limitations.

PAUL KELLY

Alexandre Izidro

The reality of domestic Mixed Martial Arts can be seen in this shot – through a boil-to-fit gumshield rather than a custom-made mouthpiece. Whilst a lot of top-tier fighters are getting high purses, good bonuses and serious sponsorship deals, there are literally thousands of lower-level fighters putting their teeth, and their health, at risk for £50 and a ticket deal.

Martin McDonough

Tom Watson

Born: November 9th, 1981
Nationality: English
Height: 5' 11"
Weight: 170lbs
Division: Welterweight
Nickname: Dre

A key upcoming Lightweight prospect in the UFC, Winner has fast hands and a natural athletic ability that enable him to maintain a ferocious pace in the cage.

Having made his way through to the finals of *The Ultimate Fighter* series, Winner found that he had to battle fellow team mate and eventual victor Ross Pearson in the finals – dispelling the myth that team mates won't fight each other. Both threw down hard and Winner's performance earned him a contract with the promotion. He then consolidated this with a highlight reel KO over former TUF contestant Rolando Delgado in Manchester at UFC 105.

Tough Japanese journeyman Daijirou Matsui is all smiles after picking up his first career submission victory – an armbar over newcomer Tom Watson.

Whist most MMA bouts take place in the cage, there are still events that take place in a ring and for many it adds a certain element of respectability to proceedings.

In Japan, the ring is king; in America the cage rules; for the M-1 Challenge event in Nottingham, 2008, it brought a breath of fresh air and an unforgiving canvass.

Dean Bray drowns his sorrows after being submitted by Ross Pointon.

In America, drinking a beer inside the cage after your fight isn't something you would get away with doing, but in the UK it's been a part of the shows for years.

Some may say it's not professional, but that said, Formula One drivers celebrate by drinking champagne ...

Chris Harman / Robert Salmon

Tom Watson / Ed Smith

Roman Webber / Mark Day

Born:	January 4th, 1974
Nationality:	English
Height:	5' 10"
Weight:	145lbs
Division:	Featherweight
Nickname:	N/A

One of the true veterans during the fledgling UK MMA scene, Batten evolved his fighting style through trial and error and a series of hard fights that were above his skill set at the time. However, he learned lessons and came through on strength of character.

Despite a career in Mixed Martial Arts that once had him ranked as high as the top Featherweight in Europe, his greatest strength is his ability to support and instruct others – imparting his knowledge to the next generation of fighters and being completely selfless in sharing his skills.

DANNY BATTEN

Adrian Jonczyk

Dan Hardy

Born: December 30th, 1984
Nationality: English
Height: 6' 2"
Weight: 170lbs
Division: Welterweight
Nickname: Slick Nick

Nick Osipczak earned his place on *The Ultimate Fighter* show
through an impressive series of tryouts and a strong elimination fight
for selection on the show. His record at the time was a budding 3–0;

Victory via head-kick KO in his first bout opened eyes, but it was his
war with DaMarques Johnson that prompted Dana White to declare
it 'one of the best fights in TUF history'. Although he lost the encounter,
his tenaciousness and display of heart secured a contract with
the promotion.

Born:	January 31st, 1978
Nationality:	English
Height:	5' 10"
Weight:	155lbs
Division:	Lightweight

Richie Downes may come across as a joker in the shot to the left of this text, but in the cage he is a very tough prospect, giving no quarter from the moment the bell rings. An unfortunate start to his pro career resulted in a loss and two no-contests, but he took a year out to refocus and has since been back in the cage picking up successive wins.

RICHIE DOWNES

With seven consecutive triangle submission victories to his credit, it's no wonder that Paul Sass currently holds the world record for the move, now dubbed the Sassangle for when he applies it.

Emmanuel Fernandez brought a halt to Paul Reed's seven-fight win-streak with a tight rear naked choke. It was a big test for the fighter at the time and showed that he could hold his own with the top talent in Europe.

As extreme as this may look – pinning someone's arm down into their own blood – understand that wrist control ensures that one offensive side of your opponent is contained, possibly allowing you to work for a submission, or hammer away with the other arm, depending on your relative body position.

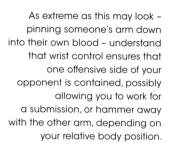

Hand injuries are all too common in MMA; some fighters are known to punch much harder than their hands allow.

The irony of having to use a tape that says 'Fragile' to secure the gloves isn't lost on me.

It's all go again, having barely had the time to get back to the locker room, take off your gloves, grab a quick sip of water and throw on a t-shirt.

You are cornering a fight, just like your team-mate did for you. Shake off the shots you took, ignore the dull pain in your thigh, take a deep breath and focus – his chance of victory depends on it.

Sergey Verdesh

Born:	December 22nd, 1986
Nationality:	English
Height:	6' 1"
Weight:	155lbs
Division:	Lightweight

An up-and-coming Lightweight fighter coming out of the Kaobon gym in Liverpool, Uche Ihiekwe's first five outings were semi-pro before he switched to full-pro rules and continued his dominance. At the time of writing he has yet to step out of the first round, blitzing his opponents with a combination of strikes and submissions, courtesy of his Luta Livre training under Marcelo Brigadeiro.

UCHE IHIEKWE

NO HOLDS BARRED

Born:	January 8th, 1982
Nationality:	American
Height:	5' 2"
Weight:	105lbs
Division:	Strawweight
Nickname:	Lil' Ice

Women's MMA is in continual ascension worldwide and the Japanese have been seasoned campaigners for many years. More recently, American-based promotions have really started to push this division's expansion, Strikeforce and Bellator being the prime movers and shakers in the US.

Jennifer Berg trains out of Grudge in Denver, Colorado, and at 105lbs is one of the future prospects to watch. She and her husband are an enthusiastic martial artists couple in their own right, and know how to push each other to succeed.

Jen got first got into Kickboxing in high school and then the Israeli art of Krav Maga; it wasn't long before she took up MMA and hasn't looked back, turning professional in 2010 with a winning debut.

Leon Roberts / Chris Rice / John Maguire

Born:	May 19th, 1983
Nationality:	English
Height:	5' 9"
Weight:	170lbs
Division:	Welterweight
Nickname:	The One

Having spent the early part of his career fighting above his natural weight class, former Middleweight champion John Maguire dropped to Welterweight after a clash with Tom Watson marked the end of his ten-fight win streak and resulted in a broken arm.

Fully recovered and with a nice shiny metal plate embedded in his forearm, Maguire has since picked up two Welterweight championship belts in different promotions: OMMAC and UCMMA. This consummate grappler has now set his sights on international promotions.

JOHN MAGUIRE

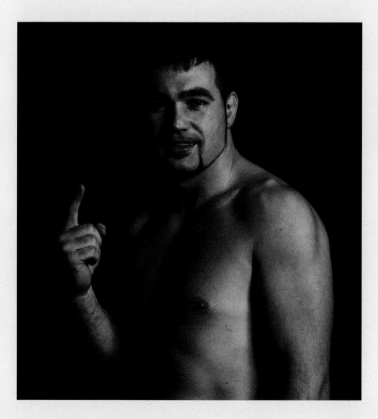

Fighting and religion have always gone hand in hand with each other, and who is to say whether your faith will protect you from the intentions of your opponent, but whatever your beliefs, faith in yourself and your abilities is the best way to guarantee safety.

Forty-five seconds between rounds barely seems long enough when you are an hour deep into a striking session at the gym.

A fresh opponent every three-minute round in continual rotation, role playing the striker, the grappler or just plain all-out MMA: training is the work – fighting is the reward.

Born:	May 10th, 1973
Nationality:	English
Height:	6' 3"
Weight:	185lbs
Division:	Middleweight
Nickname:	The Professional

Some fighters are much better than their records suggest, and Pierre Guillet is one such candidate. A full-time member of the United States military based in England, Guillet has suffered a continual mix of mistakes, bad luck and freak injuries that have contributed to a record of 11-9-1.

He is still active in the sport – but not as an active fighter; he now splits his time as a colour commentator and MMA instructor for the Team Tsunami camp.

PIERRE GUILLET

Kym Farid / Danny Cubitt

436

Born:	November 2nd, 1983
Nationality:	American
Height:	5' 7"
Weight:	145lbs
Division:	Featherweight
Nickname:	Cub

Despite having hands held together by bits of metal, Cub Swanson's unorthodox fighting style has enthralled viewers and endeared him to many fans throughout his tenure in the WEC and, formerly, KOTC promotions.

Training out of the Jackson's MMA Academy and proudly representing his Palm Springs roots, Swanson always puts on a show, be it through his behaviour in front of a camera lens, his performance in the cage or his high-speed sparring style.

Stefan Struve / Mario Neto

Frank Mir